WITHDRAWN

Why Things Don't Work
TANK

Published by Raintree, a division of Reed Elsevier, Inc.
Chicago, Illinois

Customer Service 888-363-4266
Visit our website at www.raintreelibrary.com

Why Things Don't Work TANK
was produced by

David West 🏃 **Children's Books**
7 Princeton Court
55 Felsham Road
London SW15 1AZ

Editor: Dominique Crowley
Consultant: David Willey, The Tank Museum, Bovington, England.
www.tankmuseum.org

11 10 09 08 07
10 9 8 7 6 5 4 3 2 1

Library of Congress Cataloging-in-Publication Data

West, David.
  Why things don't work. Tank / David West.
    p. cm. -- (Why things don't work)
  Includes index.
  ISBN 1-4109-2559-5
  1. Tanks (Military science)--Maintenance and repair--Juvenile literature.
  2. Tanks (Military science)--Parts--Juvenile literature. I. Title. II.
Title: Tank. III. Series: West, David. Why things don't work.
  UG446.5.W4285 2006
  623.7'4752--dc22
                                    2006017945

Printed and bound in China

Why Things Don't Work
TANK

by David West

Raintree
Chicago, Illinois

Contents

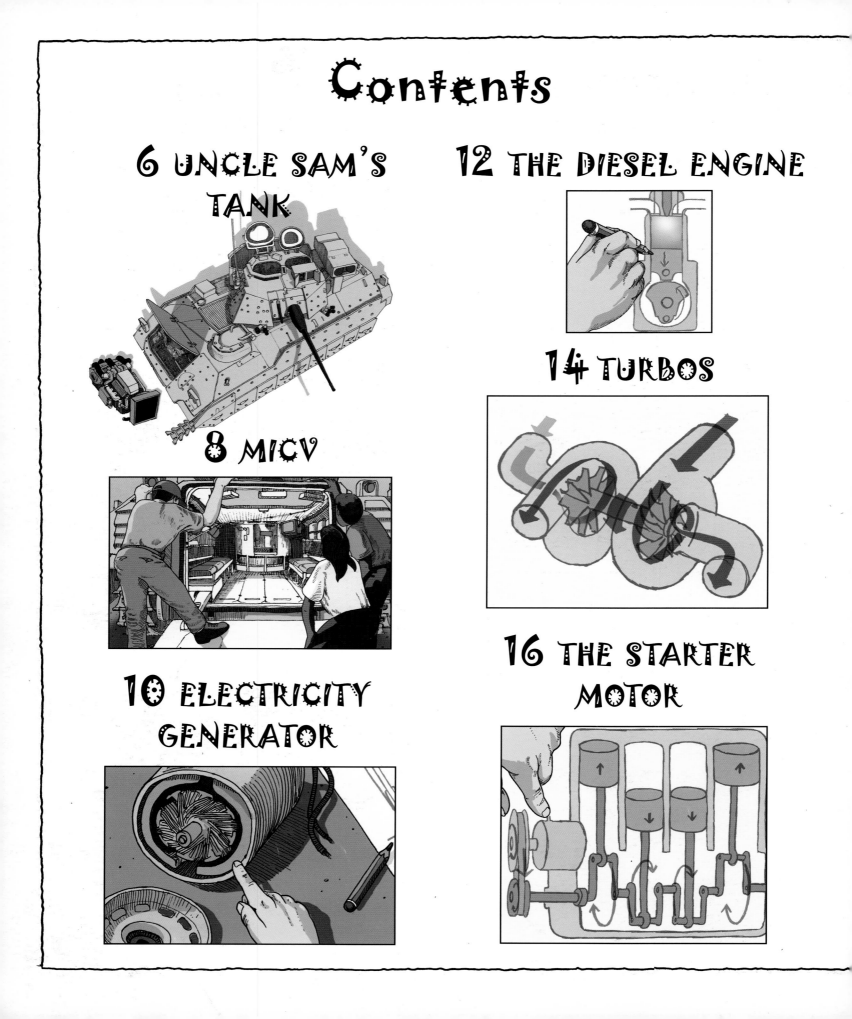

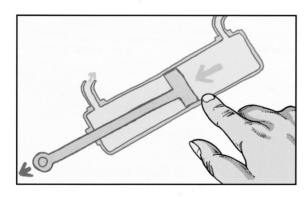

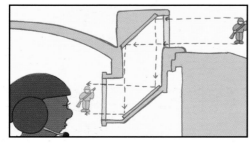

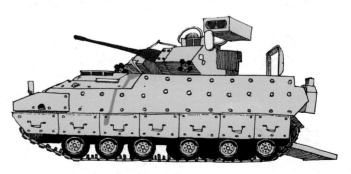

Uncle Sam's Tank

JED AND JESSICA HAVE BEEN ASKED TO HELP RESTORE THEIR UNCLE'S TANK FOR HIS MUSEUM. IF THEY GET IT FINISHED IN TIME, HE WILL LET THEM DRIVE IT AROUND THE TANK RANGE. AT THE MOMENT, THERE'S A HOLE WHERE THE ENGINE SHOULD BE.

ALSO, THERE ARE SOME OTHER PROBLEMS...

THE BATTERIES ARE DEAD.

THE ENGINE NEEDS TO BE PUT BACK INTO THE TANK.

THE CATERPILLAR TRACK IS BROKEN.

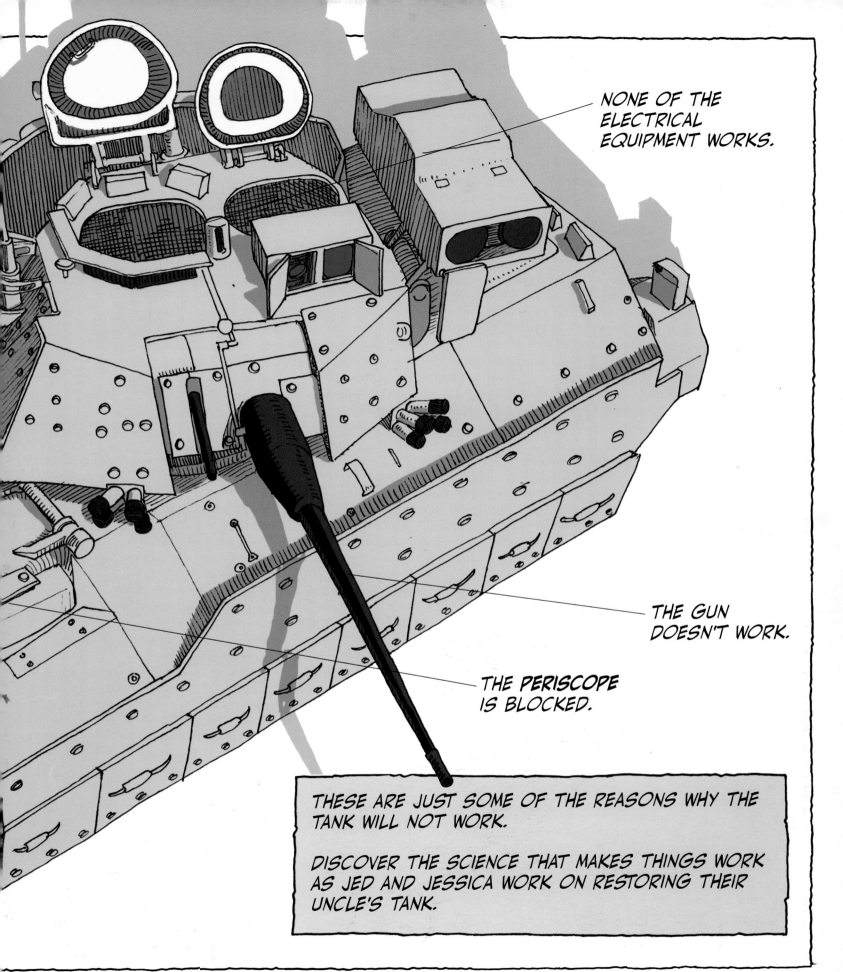

NONE OF THE ELECTRICAL EQUIPMENT WORKS.

THE GUN DOESN'T WORK.

THE PERISCOPE IS BLOCKED.

THESE ARE JUST SOME OF THE REASONS WHY THE TANK WILL NOT WORK.

DISCOVER THE SCIENCE THAT MAKES THINGS WORK AS JED AND JESSICA WORK ON RESTORING THEIR UNCLE'S TANK.

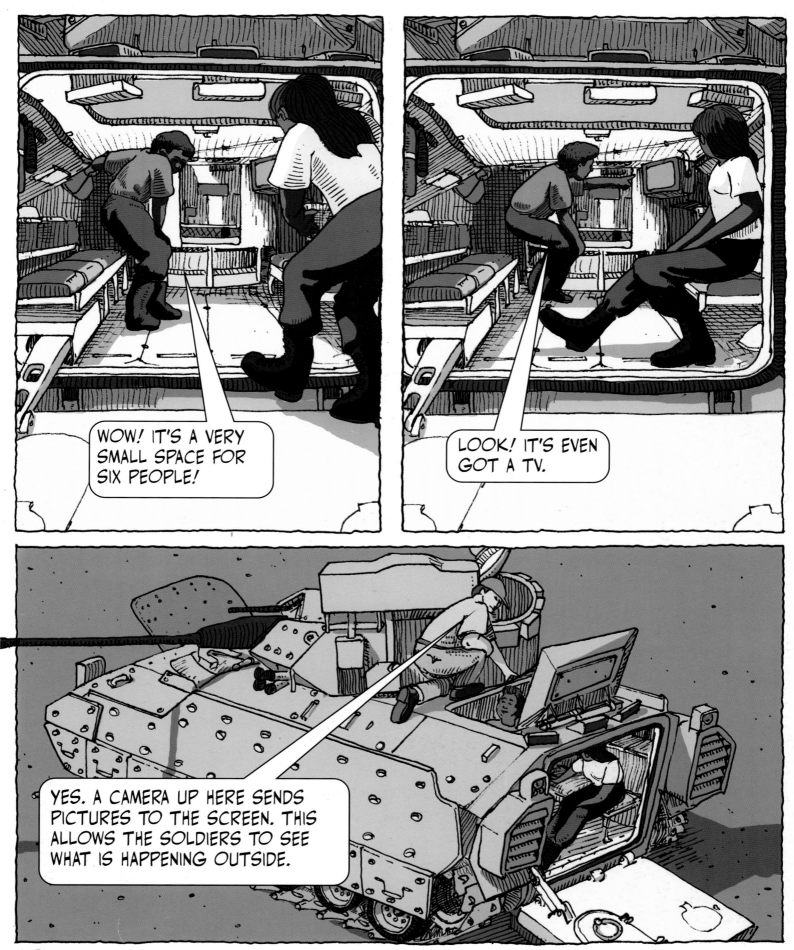

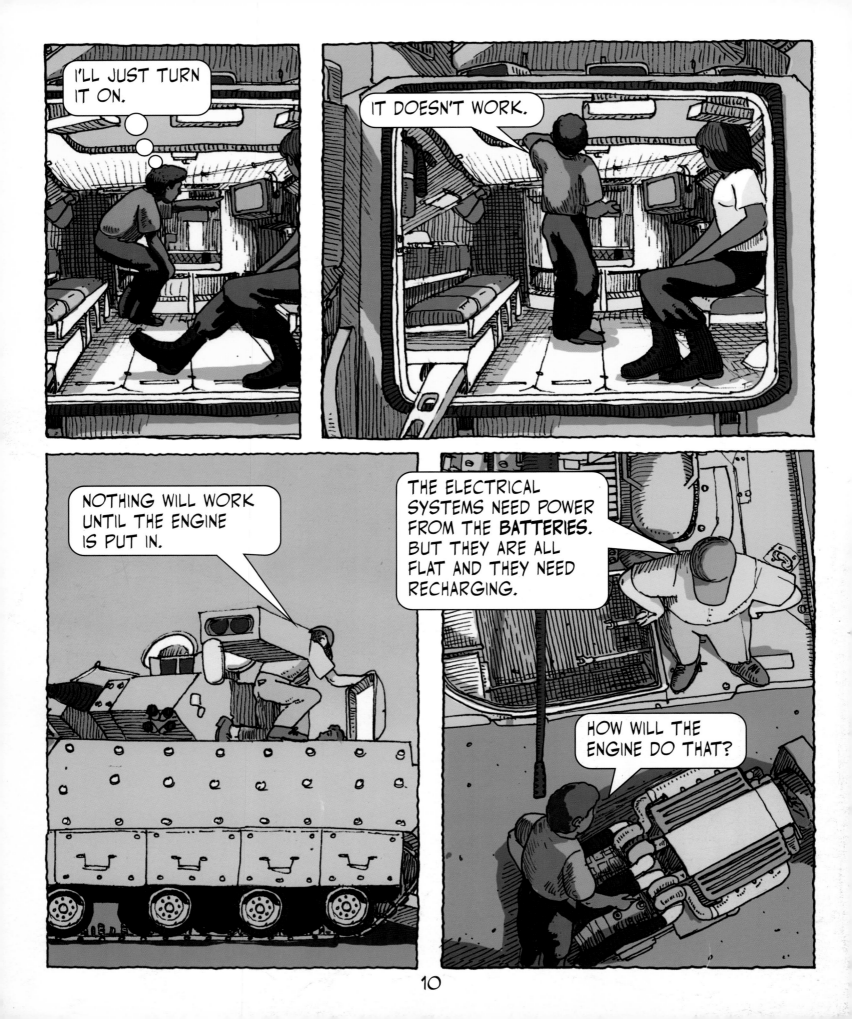

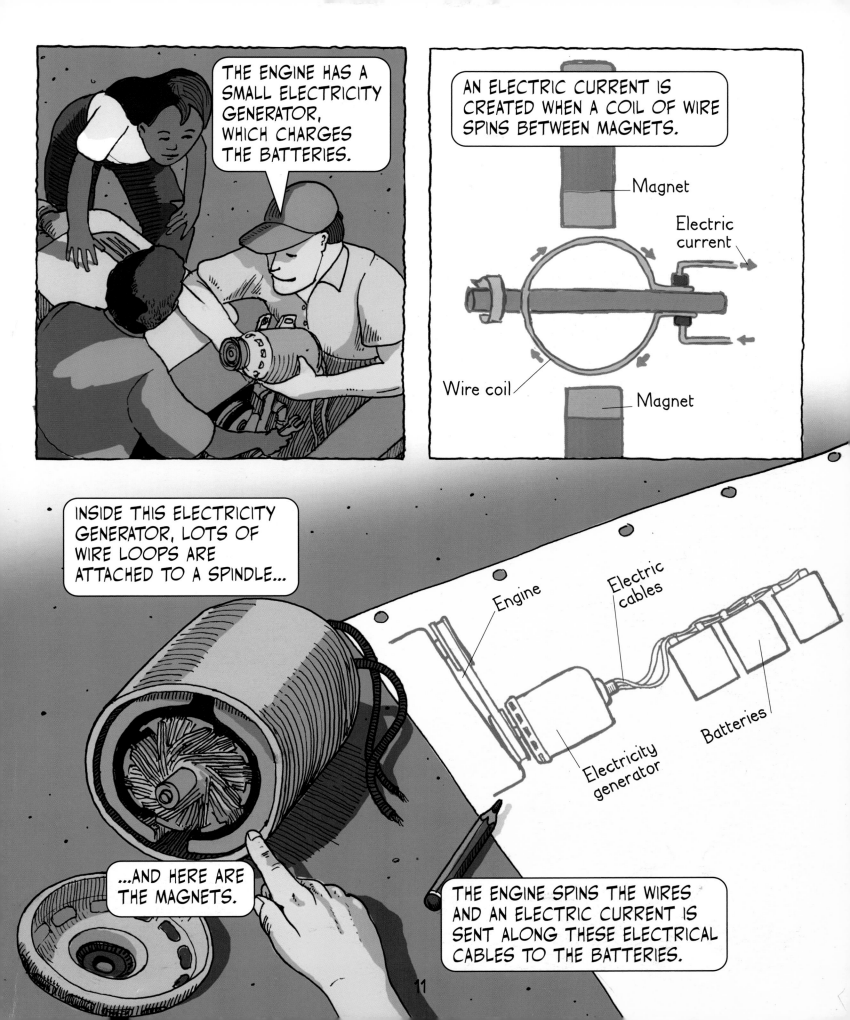

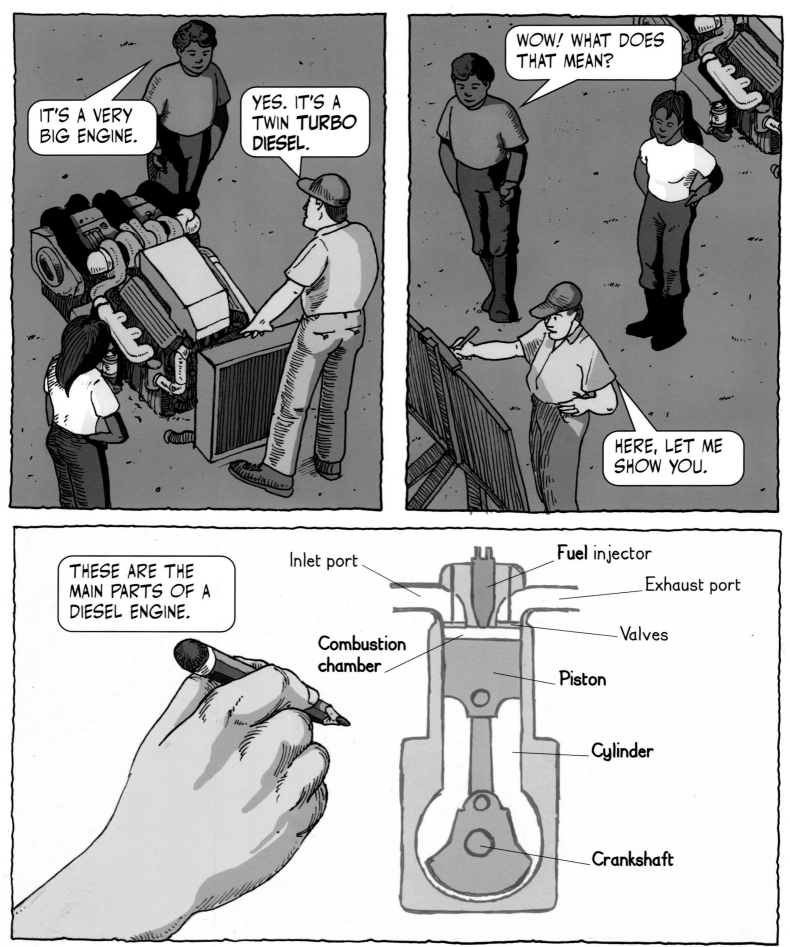

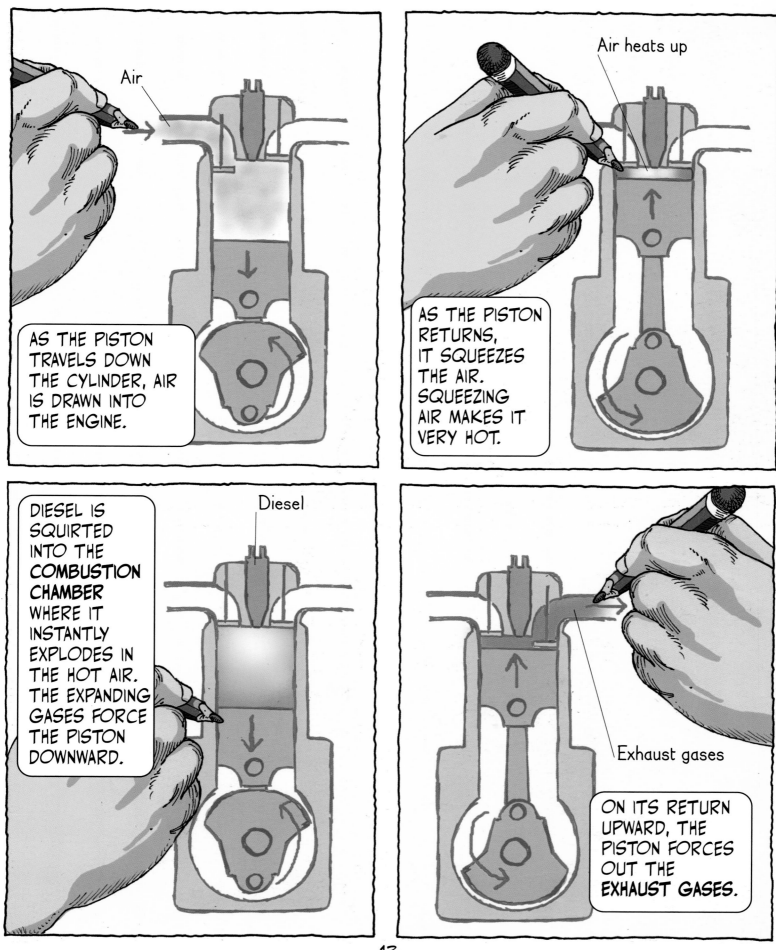

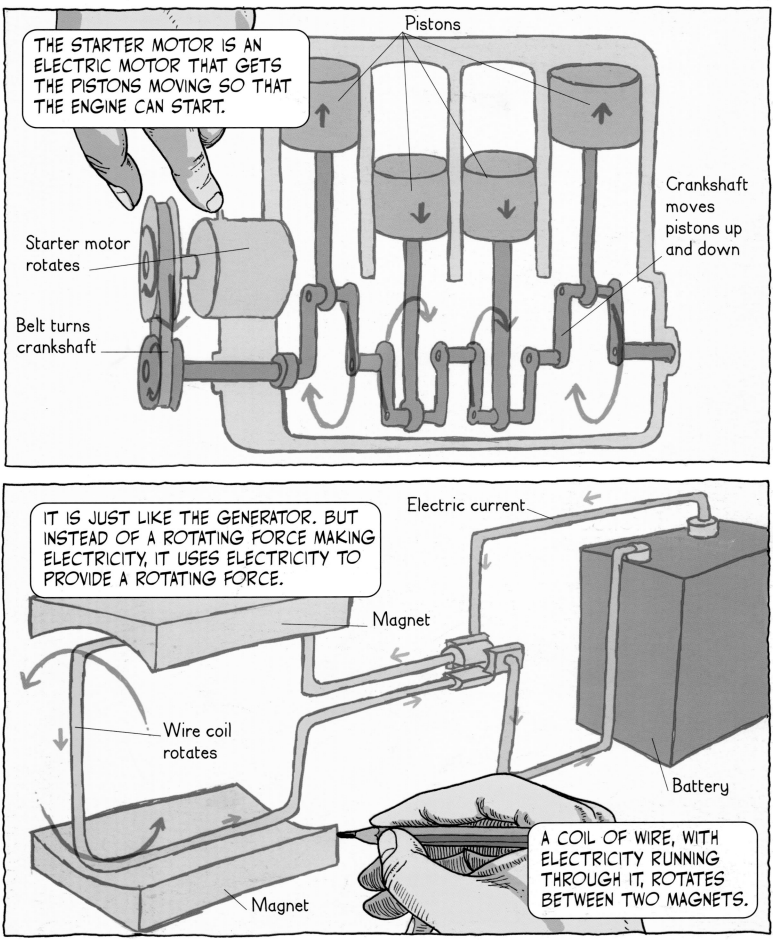

WHEN THE DRIVER TURNS THE STEERING YOLK, IT CHANGES THE AMOUNT OF POWER TO THE TWO DRIVE WHEELS.

BY TURNING IT RIGHT, THE TRACKS ON THE LEFT GO FASTER THAN THE TRACKS ON THE RIGHT. THIS MAKES THE TANK TURN RIGHT.

IN FACT, ONE TRACK CAN GO IN AN OPPOSITE DIRECTION TO THE OTHER.

THIS HELPS TO MAKE THE TANK EASY TO MANEUVER, DESPITE ITS LARGE SIZE.

WHY DO TANKS NEED CATERPILLAR TRACKS? WHY CAN'T THEY HAVE WHEELS LIKE A TRUCK?

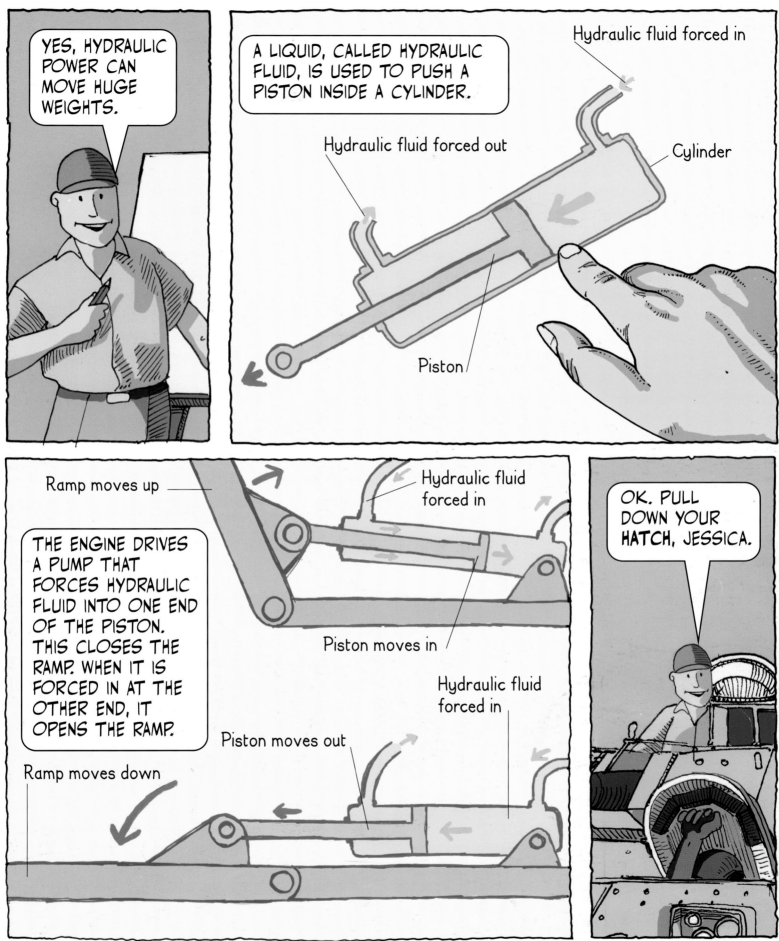

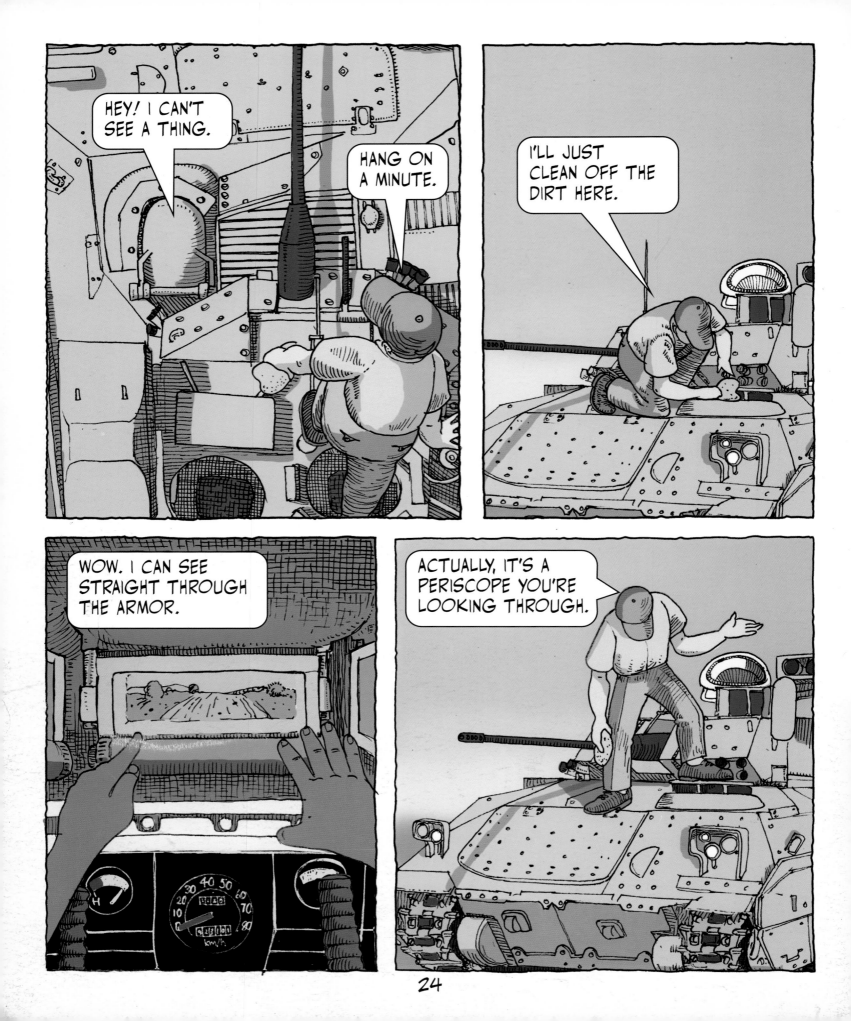

24

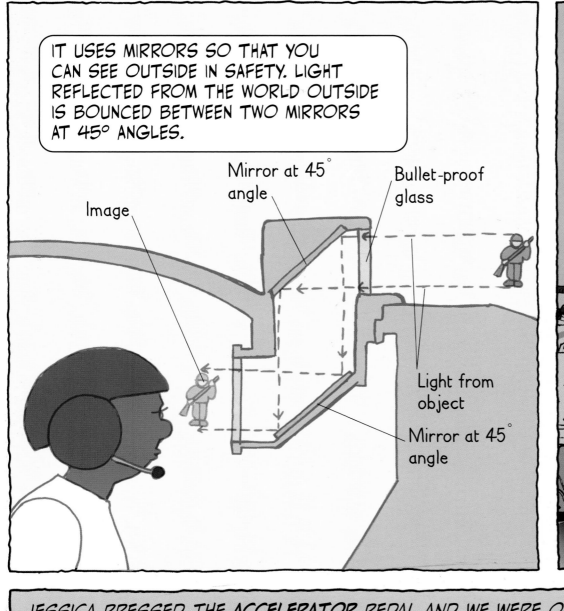

IT USES MIRRORS SO THAT YOU CAN SEE OUTSIDE IN SAFETY. LIGHT REFLECTED FROM THE WORLD OUTSIDE IS BOUNCED BETWEEN TWO MIRRORS AT 45° ANGLES.

Mirror at 45° angle

Bullet-proof glass

Image

Light from object

Mirror at 45° angle

OK, LET'S MOVE OUT.

JESSICA PRESSED THE **ACCELERATOR** PEDAL AND WE WERE OFF.

TRY TO FOLLOW THE TRACK.

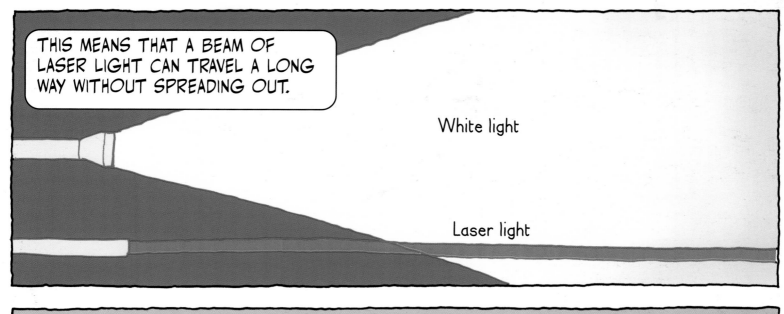

THIS MEANS THAT A BEAM OF LASER LIGHT CAN TRAVEL A LONG WAY WITHOUT SPREADING OUT.

White light

Laser light

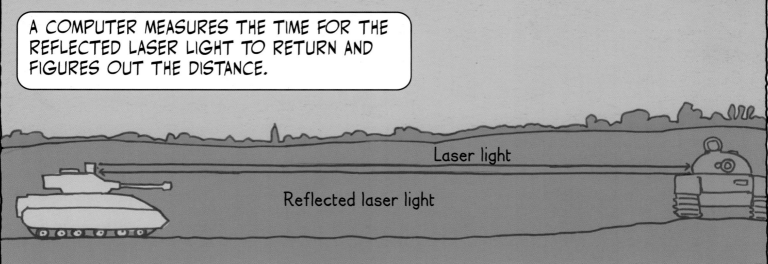

A COMPUTER MEASURES THE TIME FOR THE REFLECTED LASER LIGHT TO RETURN AND FIGURES OUT THE DISTANCE.

Laser light

Reflected laser light

WHY DOES IT NEED A LASER RANGEFINDER?

THE INFORMATION IS FED INTO A COMPUTER TO CONTROL THE GUN AND **TURRET**.

Reflected laser light

Gun

Computer

WE HAD FUN TAKING TURNS DRIVING THE TANK AROUND, BEFORE FINALLY CLEANING IT UP FOR THE MUSEUM'S DISPLAY.

THE NEXT DAY WE LOOKED AROUND UNCLE SAM'S TANK MUSEUM.

THIS IS WHAT THE FIRST TANKS LOOKED LIKE. THEY WERE USED IN WORLD WAR I.

Parts of a Tank

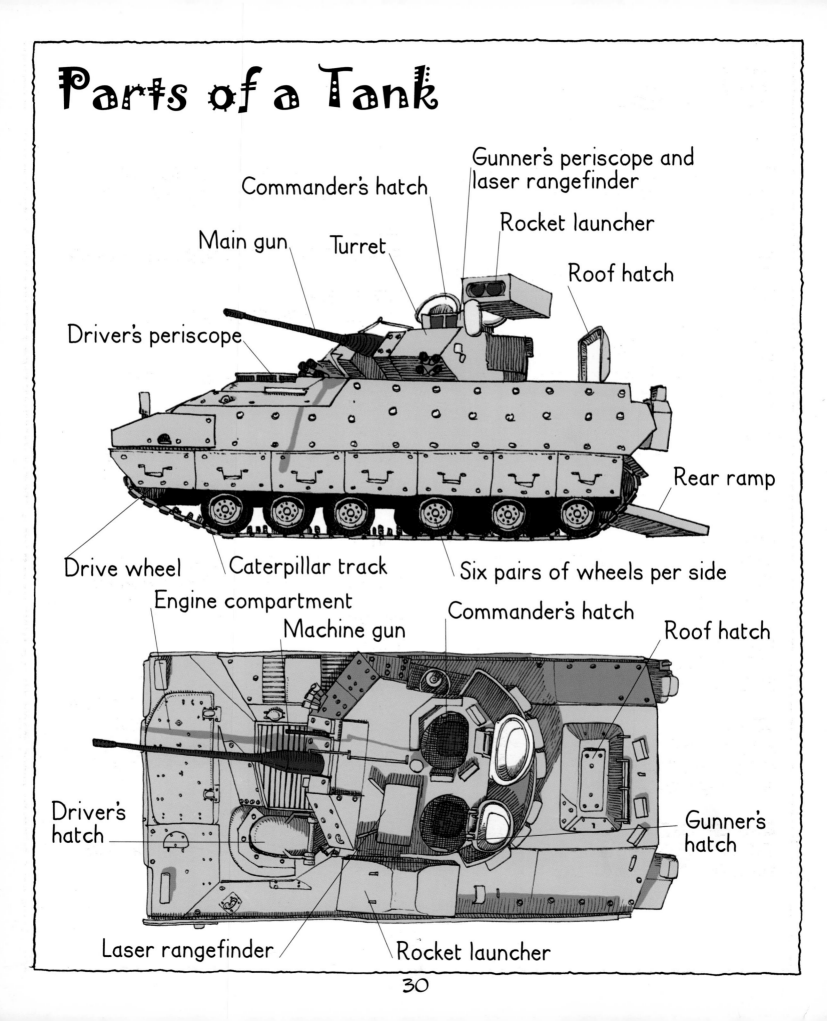

Commander's hatch

Gunner's periscope and laser rangefinder

Rocket launcher

Main gun

Turret

Roof hatch

Driver's periscope

Rear ramp

Drive wheel

Caterpillar track

Six pairs of wheels per side

Engine compartment

Machine gun

Commander's hatch

Roof hatch

Driver's hatch

Gunner's hatch

Laser rangefinder

Rocket launcher

Glossary

ACCELERATOR
THE PEDAL OR LEVER THAT CONTROLS SPEED BY CHANGING THE AMOUNT OF FUEL SUPPIED TO THE ENGINE

ARMOR
OUTER PROTECTIVE SURFACE DESIGNED TO WITHSTAND HOSTILE GUNFIRE

BATTERY
A DEVICE TO STORE ELECTRICITY. THE BATTERY PROVIDES POWER FOR THE STARTER MOTOR.

COMBUSTION CHAMBER
THE TOP PART OF THE CYLINDER WHERE THE FUEL/AIR MIXTURE IS IGNITED BY THE SPARK PLUG

CRANKSHAFT
A SHAFT THAT IS ROTATED BY THE UP AND DOWN MOVEMENT OF THE PISTONS IN AN ENGINE

CYLINDER
THE METAL SLEEVE INSIDE WHICH A PISTON MOVES

DIESEL
A TYPE OF FUEL THAT BURNS WHEN IT IS COMPRESSED AND IS DESIGNED TO WORK IN A DIESEL ENGINE

EXHAUST GASES
THE GASES CREATED BY THE EXPLODING FUEL/AIR MIXTURE IN THE ENGINE

FUEL
MATERIAL THAT IS BURNED TO GIVE POWER. TANK FUEL IS MADE FROM OIL.

HATCH
SMALL DOOR THAT COVERS AN OPENING

HYDRAULICS
PRESSURE APPLIED BY A LIQUID

INFANTRY
GROUP OF SOLDIERS WHO FIGHT ON FOOT

PERISCOPE
SYSTEM OF MIRRORS THAT ALLOWS VISION OVER OBSTACLES OR ABOVE EYE LEVEL

PISTON
A SOLID CYLINDER THAT MOVES BACK AND FORTH INSIDE ANOTHER CYLINDER

ROTATE
TURN

TURBO OR TURBOCHARGER
A DEVICE WITH TURBINES (WHEELS WITH A NUMBER OF BLADES AROUND THEIR EDGES), WHICH USES THE ENERGY PRODUCED BY EXHAUST GASES TO COMPRESS AIR

TURRET
SMALL REVOLVING TOWER ON THE TOP OF A TANK

Index